Look and Play
Jungle Animals

by Jim Pipe

Aladdin/Watts
London • Sydney

jungle

Here is a **jungle**.

lion

I see a **lion**.

5

parrot

I see a
blue **parrot**.

6

gorilla

8

A big **gorilla** sees me.

9

elephant

I see an **elephant**.

11

hippo

I see two **hippos**.

13

crocodile

14

I see a **crocodile**.
Help!

15

monkey

I see two **monkeys**.

16

snake

18

I see a **snake**.

19

Who am I?

snake

elephant

crocodile

parrot

Match the words and pictures.

How many?

Can you count the chimps?

21

What noise?

Oo! Oo! Oo!

Hiss!

Squawk!

Roar!

22

Can you sound like these animals?

Index

For Parents and Teachers

Questions you could ask:

p. 2 What can you see? Ask the reader to spot the jungle animals. Ask them to imagine what it is like living in a jungle, e.g. what is the scariest noise?

p. 4 What sound does a lion make? A lion roars. Encourage the reader to make the sound of each animal as they read through the book.

p. 6 What colours is this parrot? e.g. blue, yellow and green. Parrots come in bright colours but other jungle animals, e.g. crocodiles, are brown to help them hide or creep up on their prey.

p. 10 What is this elephant doing? It is having a drink. It sucks water up in its trunk and squirts it into its mouth! Also point out big ears and tusks.

p. 12 What are these hippos doing? They are fighting. Hippopotamuses look cuddly but in real life they are very dangerous. Point out big tusks.

p. 14 What does a crocodile's skin feel like? Its skin is tough/scaly. Compare with lion/parrot. Also point out rows of sharp teeth and long tail.

p. 16 Where do monkeys live? They spend most of their time up in trees. They are very good climbers.

p. 18 How does a snake move? It slithers – wriggling slowly along the ground/branches.

Activities you could do:

• Introduce jungle animals by singing "Five Little Monkeys", "Nellie the Elephant" and "The Animals in the Jungle" (sung to "The Wheels on the Bus") and other songs and rhymes .

• Role play: ask the reader to act out their favourite jungle animal, e.g. slithering like a snake, swinging like a monkey, snapping their jaws like a crocodile or flapping their wings like a parrot.

• Play "Catch the Snake": children form a long line holding each other at the waist. The "head" tries to catch the "tail" without breaking the line.

• On a science table, place a dish of water, a tray of dirt and a pile of grass or hay. Ask children to place plastic jungle animals in the correct habitat.

© Aladdin Books Ltd 2007

Designed and produced by
Aladdin Books Ltd
2/3 Fitzroy Mews
London W1T 6DF

First published in 2007
in Great Britain
by Franklin Watts
338 Euston Road
London NW1 3BH

Franklin Watts Australia
Level 17/207 Kent Street
Sydney NSW 2000

Franklin Watts is a division of Hachette Children's Books.

ISBN 978 0 7496 7726 8

A catalogue record for this book is available from the British Library.

Dewey Classification: 591.734

Printed in Malaysia

Series consultant
Zoe Stillwell is an experienced Early Years teacher currently teaching at Pewley Down Infant School, Guildford.

Photocredits:
l-left, r-right, b-bottom, t-top, c-centre, m-middle
All photos on cover and insides from istockphoto.com except:
23tl, mrt & rb — Ingram.
22bl — John Foxx.